U.S. NATIONAL PARKS
GREAT SMOKY MOUNTAINS
NATIONAL PARK

by Penelope S. Nelson

Ideas for Parents and Teachers

Pogo Books let children practice reading informational text while introducing them to nonfiction features such as headings, labels, sidebars, maps, and diagrams, as well as a table of contents, glossary, and index.

Carefully leveled text with a strong photo match offers early fluent readers the support they need to succeed.

Before Reading

- "Walk" through the book and point out the various nonfiction features. Ask the student what purpose each feature serves.
- Look at the glossary together. Read and discuss the words.

Read the Book

- Have the child read the book independently.
- Invite him or her to list questions that arise from reading.

After Reading

- Discuss the child's questions. Talk about how he or she might find answers to those questions.
- Prompt the child to think more. Ask: Many people see the Great Smoky Mountains from their cars. Others like to hike. Which would you prefer? Why?

Pogo Books are published by Jump!
5357 Penn Avenue South
Minneapolis, MN 55419
www.jumplibrary.com

Copyright © 2020 Jump!
International copyright reserved in all countries. No part of this book may be reproduced in any form without written permission from the publisher.

Library of Congress Cataloging-in-Publication Data

Names: Nelson, Penelope, 1994– author.
Title: Great Smoky Mountains National Park by Penelope S. Nelson.
Description: Minneapolis, MN: Jump!, 2020.
Series: U.S. national parks | "Pogo Books."
Includes index.
Identifiers: LCCN 2018052601 (print)
LCCN 2018053092 (ebook)
ISBN 9781641288149 (ebook)
ISBN 9781641288132 (hardcover : alk. paper)
Subjects: LCSH: Great Smoky Mountains National Park (N.C. and Tenn.) –Juvenile literature.
Classification: LCC F443.G7 (ebook)
LCC F443.G7 N45 2020 (print) | DDC 976.8/89–dc23
LC record available at https://lccn.loc.gov/2018052601

Editor: Jenna Trnka
Designer: Jenna Casura

Photo Credits: KenCanning/iStock, cover; Dean_Fikar/iStock, 1; CrackerClips/iStock, 3; Michael Warren/iStock, 4; Pat & Chuck Blackley/Alamy, 5; alex grichenko/iStock, 6-7; Jon Bilous/Shutterstock, 8-9; Betty4240/iStock, 10-11; SeanPavonePhoto/iStock, 12, 14-15; PhotosbyAndy/iStock, 13; Zoonar GmbH/Alamy, 16; WendyOlsenPhotography/iStock, 17; NaturalStock/Shutterstock, 18-19; Oliver Gerhard/Alamy, 20-21; smartstock/iStock, 23.

Printed in the United States of America at Corporate Graphics in North Mankato, Minnesota.

TABLE OF CONTENTS

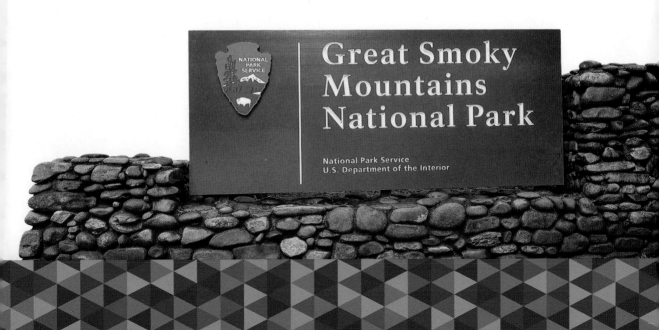

NATIONAL PARK SERVICE

Great Smoky
Mountains
National Park

National Park Service
U.S. Department of the Interior

CHAPTER 1

BEAUTIFUL MOUNTAINS

Would you like to see more than 1,500 types of wildflowers?

Maybe you want to fish for trout. You would love Great Smoky Mountains National Park!

This national park is in North Carolina and Tennessee. It is made up of the Great Smoky Mountains. It was founded in 1934. Why? The government wanted to protect the land, plants, and animals here.

DID YOU KNOW?

How did these mountains get their name? The many trees and plants in the mountains release water **vapor**. It looks like smoke. Native Americans saw it. They called the area Shaconage. This means "land of the blue smoke."

Logging and farming were once popular **industries** in this area. You can still visit **mills**. See how grain was ground in the early 1900s at Mingus Mill.

Nearby, Mountain Farm Museum shows historic gardening and farming. There is a working **blacksmith** shop, too!

WHAT DO YOU THINK?

Logging is not allowed in these mountains anymore. Do you think it should be allowed? Why or why not?

Mingus Mill

church

Almost 100 historic buildings are here! See cabins and churches. Explore schools. Some are in Cataloochee Valley. Others are in Cades Cove. You can tour these old towns!

DID YOU KNOW?

More than 150 graveyards are in the park! They total more than 4,500 graves!

CHAPTER 2
WOODED LANDSCAPE

Ecosystems here include **wetlands**. The park is mostly forest. Find more than 100 types of trees here.

wetlands

The **climate** is **temperate**. Animals have **adapted** to the weather changes each season. You could see a black bear! Keep your distance!

The **peaks** and valleys of the mountains create incredible sights. Clingmans Dome is the highest point in the park. How high is it? It is 6,643 feet (2,025 meters)! Newfound Gap is the lowest **pass**. You can drive through it!

Newfound Gap

TAKE A LOOK!

The Great Smoky Mountains are part of the Appalachian Mountains. This chain stretches down the eastern United States. What are some of the parts of a mountain called?

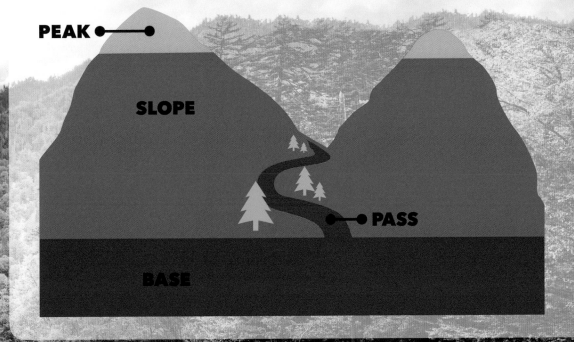

PEAK

SLOPE

PASS

BASE

CHAPTER 3

SIGHTS TO SEE

Hiking is a great way to see this park! Many trails will take you to see waterfalls, like Grotto Falls. Mount Cammerer Trail ends with a lookout tower. It was originally used to spot wildfires!

lookout tower

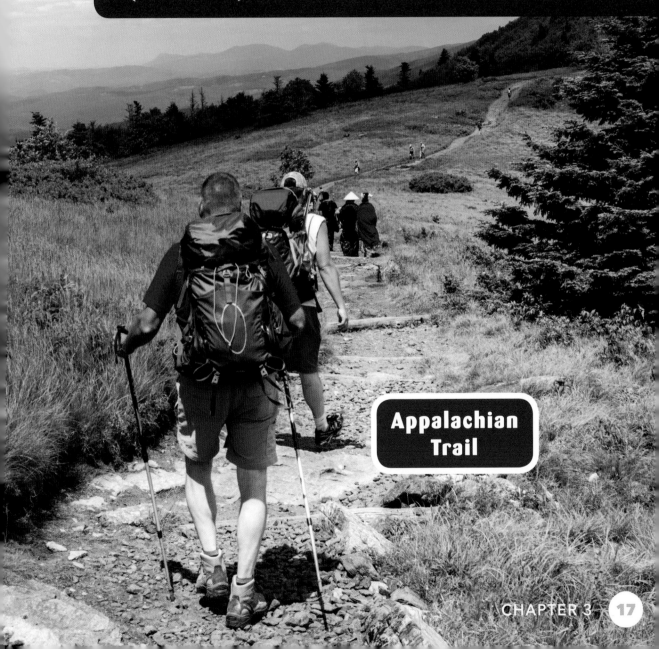

About 70 miles (113 kilometers) of the Appalachian Trail runs through the park. This trail spans about 2,200 miles (3,541 km) of the eastern United States.

Appalachian Trail

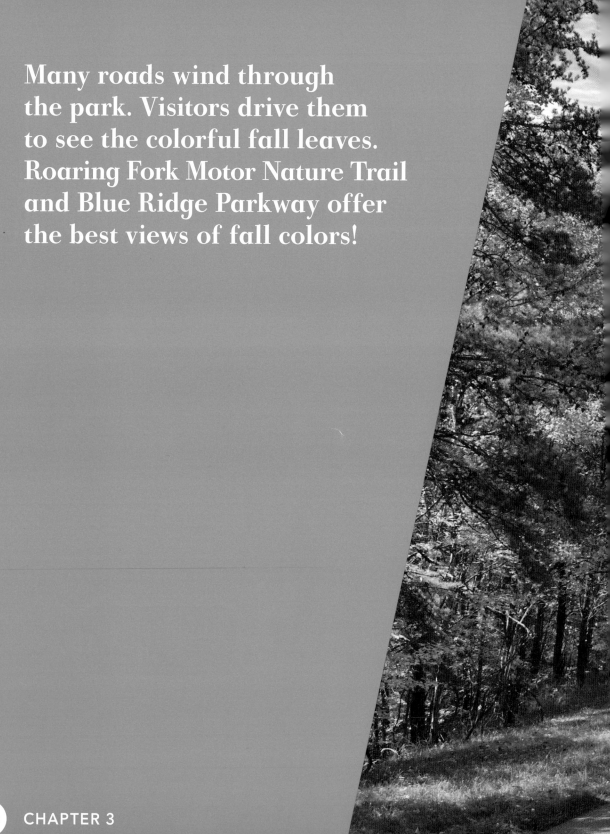

Many roads wind through the park. Visitors drive them to see the colorful fall leaves. Roaring Fork Motor Nature Trail and Blue Ridge Parkway offer the best views of fall colors!

LeConte Lodge

Visitors looking to stay overnight can camp in the park! LeConte Lodge is another place to stay. You can only get here by hiking. Then you can stay in an old-fashioned log cabin!

Great Smoky Mountains National Park is full of natural beauty! What would you like to see?

WHAT DO YOU THINK?

Would you rather stay in a cabin or camp in a tent? Why?

QUICK FACTS & TOOLS

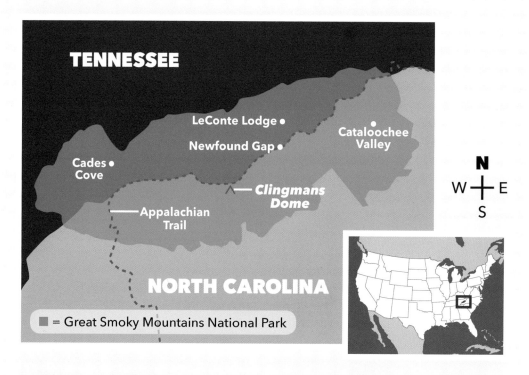

TENNESSEE

LeConte Lodge ●

Cataloochee Valley ●

Newfound Gap ●

Cades Cove ●

∧— *Clingmans Dome*

— Appalachian Trail

NORTH CAROLINA

N
W ✛ E
S

■ = Great Smoky Mountains National Park

GREAT SMOKY MOUNTAINS NATIONAL PARK

Location: North Carolina and Tennessee

Year Established: 1934

Area: 522,427 acres (211,419 hectares)

Approximate Yearly Visitors: 11 million

Top Attractions: Cades Cove, Clingmans Dome, Newfound Gap

Total Length of Hiking Trails: 850 miles (1,368 kilometers)

GLOSSARY

adapted: Changed to suit a different situation.

blacksmith: Someone who makes things by heating and bending iron.

climate: The weather typical of a place over a long period of time.

ecosystems: Areas that include all of the living and nonliving things within them.

industries: Branches of business or trade.

logging: The act of clearing trees and cutting them for lumber.

mills: Buildings that contain the machinery to grind grain into flour.

pass: A low place in a mountain range.

peaks: The pointed tops of high mountains.

temperate: A climate that rarely has very high or very low temperatures.

vapor: Fine particles of mist, steam, or smoke that can be seen hanging in the air.

wetlands: Marshy and wet areas of land.

INDEX

TO LEARN MORE

Finding more information is as easy as 1, 2, 3.

❶ Go to www.factsurfer.com

❷ Enter "GreatSmokyMountainsNationalPark" into the search box.

❸ Choose your book to see a list of websites.

FACT SURFER